Dedications

This book is dedicated to the number one in my life God first, and foremost. I would like to Thank my late Grandmother Julia B. Noble. I asked was she proud of me for the song I sang in church, and she replied; I was proud of you the day you were born: Thank you Granny I've never forgotten. Along with the knowledge no one else felt to give me, (I Love You). To my also Late Mother Dinah B. Poe even though she is not here in physical form she is still in my heart giving me the strength to hold on. I would also like to give thanks to my husband Dennis J. Conner for being there for me, believing in me, and being my back bone; when I wanted to give up. Giving thanks to my Children for giving me the courage to live and be able to write this book: without them I would not know my own strength. Thank you babies and there is more to come. My favorite teacher and friend Janet Tackett a true teacher and woman of God. Last, but not least I would like to thank my truly loyal sister Keisha Chavers wo introduced me to the mic and watched me grow to maturity; Thanks a million Sis.

Publisher's Info:

NTLP Potter Publishing, LLC

P.O. Box 602711

Cleveland, Ohio 44102

Phone: (216) 282-5433

Contents

1. I Will Be Victorious
2. Do You Hear the Sista's Cry?
3. God is Drawing His People
4. Teach Me How to Let Go
5. Children Where Are You
6. Help Me Be Still
7. Heart to Heart
8. If you hadn't Reached Me First
9. May I lay at Your Feet
10. Intimate Struggles
11. Does this Mean
12. Just Keep Me Going
13. My Vision and Me
14. This is the Day
15. I Don't Receive It
16. What's Change
17. Not in My Own Strength
18. Ready to Say Good-Bye
19. Women Don't Settle for Less
20. Lord I'm Almost
21. Am I speaking from My heart
22. Draw Me again I pray
23. Sometimes I need You More
24. Keep on, Keepin On
25. Just Envision
26. If I let, Go Now
27. Leave Her Alone She's My Child
28. Praise the Lord Your God
29. I Need You to Survive
30. Are The Rocks Crying Out?
31. Many Let Go's
32. I'll Wait for My Mate
33. How Much More Lord
34. Just What Are You Trying to Say to Me
35. Beginning with Me

I will be victorious spoke on overcoming the hardships of a once defeated life. The defeated was no longer the victim of a life of the whispers of the defeater's voices that spoke in the corners of a beings' soul; with words that took root. Generational curses that followed the defeated; as well as, the persecutions of those curses spoken over them. There were times bitterness would creep in, because of the death of my mother, and never receiving understanding of her death why? Did this happen to me. Disaster seemed to wait for me to step out of the front door; as though it was a friend knocking waiting for me to answer and then dragging me in the middle of the street to fight a battle that was staged set for my demise. Going through this I still felt the presence of the anointing of God though not knowing that it was there to feed me how to love the individuals that fragmented me he allowed my hurt to not override the love that resided in my heart. The times that I sat in church and heard sermons of love preached over the pulpit; as well as the forgiveness that we should practice 70x7 from the King James and off the the lips of my first spiritual father great teacher that still have to this day influenced the decisions I make. He was such a great example to me. The way he lived his life, but I know God placed him in my life even being that young. He was one of my teachers that showed e how to live for the Lord. In my circle of people; that didn't give me what I needed to carry on and through the man of God my tears are sweet to him a sweet smelling savor. I was enough for him to go to the cross and shed his blood to fight for me when no one else found me suitable. He called me his child; I' the one he loves and he's mine and I'm his this is why I will be victorious, because my God lives. This alone expressed how the love of my pastor was shown through that and revealed God and his presence to me. I saw God in this very that I began to seek God for myself, and build a spiritual relationship that helped me to identify with what was being fed into my spirit, and I knew that persecution and no matter how I was treated; nor what was said I was given the tools in my life and in my spirit to fight what was knocking at my door. To go out blazing with the holy spirit teaching me. I believe and I know that I can make it, I know that I can stand, God is my confidence he's my one and only man. I will be victorious, because of m God he leads me around and he doesn't allow me to be bound. He gives me strength when I am weak I'm his honey and he's so ever sweet. I knew at this point my life was being turned around. I will be victorious spoke of me coming out of the wilderness.

I Will Be Victorious

I will be victorious, because of who I am. I once was lost and my life what just a jam. I could not get past the bitter hatred in order to strive for what I wanted the many trials, the tribulations, the hurts, the pains, all the bad manifestations. I believe and I know that I can make it, I know that I can stand. God is my confidence he is my one and only man. I will be victorious, because of my God he leads me around and he doesn't allow me to be bound. He gives me strength when I am weak, I'm his honey and he's so ever sweet. He lets me know when I'm wrong. He lets me feel when he's there. I'm on a new road with him and better things are coming my way; no hurt, no harm, no rejection from my God; for he loves me and he alone. I never knew love until I met him. I dibbled and dabbled in his presence, but with him is where I want to be still. He's wonderful he's wonderful you know he's a GOD ON HIGH AND A GOD I CAN'T DENY! He teaches me how to love and that's what I want to do, feel his touch ad tender mercies, his touch is warm, his love for me is great. This I never experienced it's just so good and slap of love in my face. This is why I know that I will be victorious, and because of the God I serve: my tears are sweet to him to go to the cross and shed his blood and fight for me when no one else found me suitable, he called me his child. I'm the one he loves and he's mine and I'm his this is why I will be victorious because MY GOD LIVES!!!

Do You hear the sista's cry speaks on behalf of all women that stood their grounds as a mother and a woman; when the strength of the man that we thought we had did not fulfill the shoes he tried on, but let the woman to do so herself. This piece bellowed out P.U.S.H within a determined woman. She put those shoes on that the man left and for some time she walked around in shoes that were to big for her and they flapped, because she to was unable to carry this load, but as time went on she found ways to make them fit, to stop the flapping they have learned to lace up those boots for a better fit and as time went on we learned how to fill them. I can say that for me the reason that I was in a lot of adultery, fornicating, and love ventures was that spun me into wedlock with no idea or intent of having multiple children by separate father's and not believing in abortion; being gullible with a heart worn on the sleeve of a bright white t-shirt. I still wanted to find the physical touch that I was use to; the hugs and closeness of my mother. I looked for from men to snuggle up with; only it was a lot more than the touch of a mother that filtered through older men and spiraled throughout my life. Looking for affection and I'm not sure if I liked the touch and feel of the men that would feel me up, but through that I learned it was a touch that would give me what I was missing. I don't know even if the sex I experienced with my first love was acknowledged until I realized the affection that came along with it. I quickly learned that the touch the feel the motion of making love was more of the feeling: I thought I needed. I knew God could not be replaced he was my rock, my solid assurance for morality, my reason for living until I had my children who were also a physical form of Love, but god could not physically touch me, nor hold me the way a man could or even a small child. When their tiny arms and hands would embrace my face and my neck; so I thought. So now this emptiness I had been feeling all this time since, the newness of the touch that I had been longing for had took me over the edge and with the education of men 101 from my grandmother. I learned how not to get attached, but I didn't want my children growing up without a father, but was willing to put on those boots if need be, but with the awareness of the possibility of me raising them on my own, but for the touch, the feel of affection it seemed worth it. One baby, two baby, three baby, four, five baby, six baby, know not talking about Christmas cause that's beauty that glisten, but letting everyone know that God had nothing to do with my down fall. God and the

Gov. which is not in comparison of one another to me, but yet they were what kept me afloat in a lot of ways. I was willing to give compromises to black men for them to step into their manhood. I come to you in honesty not a nice cold beer, that line was written to take men the father's out of their comfort zone and face their responsibility. Sexual relations were not all that we desired with them something more was nudging us. The protection, security, and the love of a man. The yelling of the poem is an effort to get the attention. You don't examine our hearts mostly you hit us with another blow. Do you hear the Sista's cry is a reaching out to men for their love and support?

Do You Hear the Sista's Cry?

Help! Is what we yell from the mountain tops of our hearts,
Do you hear the sista's cry? From the youngest to the oldest all races are involved. Their not one sista that don't yell and has the desire to be held not by our hips or with your fingertips, but held with an untouched love that's Where Love starts!

We cry out night and day not that you hear our cry, from thoughts of filth on the bay. WHY make the baby that's not yours so you say? don't try and escape being a daddy thinking a blood test would put a longer delay. When we wrestle with our emotions of Hurt, bitterness, and rebellion; then you get mad when we become a hellion. We've grown
up some since you last saw us love us, or leave my sista and I be. I don't cry out for just me it's me and my sista so they won't be in this twista.

Help! Help! is what we yell do you hear the sista's cry? If you listen close, you'll hear stress and our eyes are not dry. I scream out loud cause that's the only way you'll listen. I'm not talkin about CHRISTmas, cause that's beauty that glistens, this is a cry of pain my brother's heart is the one to gain, not to have red hot sex, but to put my hand in yours and know that it's only us you adore. There's strong sista's in this world of war get one like you or that's torn down and build her up and know that you both drunk from the same cup.

Can you feel me then answer? We call you by your first name, you call us something that Doesn't even represent, to know the depths of hurt let's share our hurt and start with just little spurts. Do you hear the sista's cry? When you plant your seed if a baby is coming just then take heed. You were man enough to lay down so be a father and succeed. The mother left to a job alone then when the child becomes rich you want a piece of the bone.

I've expressed myself the best way I know how. The question I want to know is; Do you hear the sista's cry? The government does they do all they can; it's you my superstar strong man hear me loud and clear I come to you in honesty not a nice cold beer. Can you hear me? can you feel me? If you do, then answer that's the only way I'll know your true Love This is where it will begin to show you want to know why?

We trip you don't examine our hearts mostly you hit us with another blow. Those hits are hard and weigh about 2 tons this is a part of life we can't count as fun. Let's begin out jobs and do what is right let's not start tomorrow, but Let's start tonight.

God is drawing his people speaks of the change that will come to Cleveland, because the prayer and the fasting that is being practiced by his children that serve him. The gates are a symbolization of that which the people have exercised freeing themselves of the sin and acts of fornication and etc. The cities are the minds of the people that are asking God to cleanse them and clean them up. The gates are the openings to the cities: the eyes, ears, nose, and other bodily parts that are used to develop Soul ties godly and ungodly.

God Is Drawing His People

We've constantly prayed Lord send souls from the North, South,
East, and West. John Ch.16 V.23 says anything you ask the
Father in Jesus Name he will give it to you.

Believe in his word and he will see you through. When the Lord is
Ready to move we give up without doing our best.
Proverbs ch.13 V.4 A lazy person craves food when there is none,
But the appetite of hard-working people is satisfied.

This is the time God wants to draw not our time. It's not our time it's
his Proverbs Ch.14 V.12 there is a way that seemeth right unto man,
but
The end thereof are the ways of death. We were made to bring the
good
News not give up so JESUS WON'T LOOSE.

This will be the new city of God:
The North side will be 7,875 feet long. The gates of the city will be
named after the tribes of Israel. The three gates on the North side will
be Rueben Gate, Judah gate and Levi gate.

The East side will be 7,875 feet long. The three gates on the East side
will Be Joseph gate, Benjamin gate, and Dan gate, The South side will
be 7,875 feet long. The three gates on the South side will be Simeon
gate, Issachar gate, and Zebulun gate.

The West side will be 7,875 feet long. The three gates on the West side
will Be Gad gate, Asher gate, and Naphtali gate. The city will measure

about 31,500 feet all the way around. From then on the city's name will be:

THE LORD IS THERE. (sayeth the Holy Bible)

Is what the new city of Cleveland will be.

Let's begin our jobs and do what is right let's not start tomorrow, but Let's start tonight.

<u>Teach Me How To Let Go</u>

As many times as I cried out
Lord help me! I know you hear, but unless I
forgive those that have hurt me and put me under
that I will forgive them; as well as myself.

Lord I feel as though my heart is so heavily wounded, beat
down, and hurt; that I can't move on.
I feel as though my life is at a standstill and though when
I pray.
I know you hear and I feel your presence,
But still I'm ashamed to speak to you.

Even though your word says you forgive and it's
thrown into the sea of forgetfulness
my heart is still burdened and
heavy Lord Please! Deliver me.

When I walk by certain someone's I still feel the same
grudge and the tear in my heart, though those people may or may not
know Lord I
do so please! Teach me how to let go.

Children Where Are You extends a hand to our children, and show them that there is a better way out. It speaks of the things we did as children; playing games, duck duck goose, freeze tag, red light, green light, one, two, three, it made me think of things that I did as a child; making mud pies when the toys were outdated for us for our entertainment. We used the earth for fun; mud, grass, and water to be a pie; rocks for nuts. Children are often taken advantage of, because they are left unprotected in so many areas: their innocence is violated, brought on by people who see our children as targets to express their demons and go free. Standing on the corner selling your dope or running for the big man. Holding your gat thinking you must stay strapped, girls putting on lipstick. We must be a guiding light for the children of this world all races need to be shielded. God loves all little children he says in his word forbid them not to come unto him. In his word he says to come to him as a child. At some point we have to see that our children are targeted for a spiritual attack we must give our children a positive way or outlet reach out to them, because they are our future: "a child shall lead them" I called out your name, but you didn't answer so I stopped playing the game. I went in the house thought about what you're going through all the hurts, fears, and the doubts. Things are conquered through prayer. We must watch and pray; redirect our children. When we feel like we are not off kilter; take a step back and regroup your thoughts. Come out with a clean directed plan. This is the reason for Children Where Are You!

Children Where Are You?

Come out! Come out! Wherever you are; I know your hiding
and I'm trying to find you, we played so many games peek-a-boo
and I see you.

Here's another one duck duck goose; I really liked freeze tag; red
light, green light, one, two, three. Children Where Are You? Hiding
in your anger? Well that just shouldn't be.

Hello Children, Children Where Are You? I called out your name,
but you didn't answer so I stopped playing the game. I went in the
house thought about what you're going through all the
hurts, fears, and the doubts.

Standing on the corner selling your dope or running for the big man,
Children come out I'll be your friend and hold your hand.
Holding your gat thinking you must stay strapped that's only in your
mind that your trapped.

making mud pies; at the age of thirteen your face should be where
your school book lies. Children Where Are You? You can be free!
We'll play more games put your mind in a different frame.

**HATRED IS WEAK, BUT LOVE IS STRONG. CHILDREN
COME OUT WITH JESUS WE CAN GO WRONG.**

Help Me be still being about a young lady that had not established stability nor a foundation. She would move to one place stay for a year or so if that long; then jump to another state whichever way that the wind would blow In between her moving and stay with different people and their families from one state to another. She met people her children father and was producing children along the way not that this young lady has three young girls with no help from any of the childrens' father's. She realizes she needs stability, a place that is steady that her children can call home, have warm meals, and a place to lay their head for refugee. Awakened by this reality she reaches out to God and ask him to help her be still when she recognizes what she needs out of life and what future she wants to leave for them. This young lady knew that she was running from her past, gossiping of others and mothers of the church on how she lived her life judgment of having babies out of wedlock, not having the best of things, lacking support of loved ones who wanted to see her down fall. Make my enemy who is on my caboose, Father make him let loose, let loose. I don't want to run off get into sin and make like it's fun, when I have a God on high; looking to the hills from which cometh my help. Once she came to know that she ask God for anything, she began to ask God to fight her enemies for her, because they didn't want what was best for her so she asked God to do for her what he gave David the courage to do. Cut off my enemies and let me fight or you could do it if that would be alright. Help me be still was an effective prayer in this young ladies life ask and it all shall be given unto you.

<u>Help Me Be Still</u>

Father, In the name of Jesus teach me how to be still.
I'm asking you this, because I know your real.

You said in John Ch.16 V.24 anything I ask the Father
In the name of Jesus you would fulfill the task.

Make my enemy who is on my caboose, Father make him
let loose, let loose. I don't want to run off get into sin and make
like it's fun, when I have a God on high; that sits on the throne
and he doesn't use a cave man's Bone.

Cut off my enemy and let me fight or you could do it if that would
be alright, in Psalms Ch.23 V.5 you said you prepare a table
banquet for me while my enemies watch.

In Samuel Ch.17 V.1-58 you gave David victory so can you do it
for me. Cut off my enemies head and make him let me be let me sit
still sit still I KNOW YOU WILL, BECAUSE YOU MY GOD ARE
REAL.

THANK YOU LORD I GIVE PRAISE!!

This poem was written to test who was really in control and my father
was more than just Faithful.

Heart to Heart is just giving back to pastors that has made room for us in their life to share with us the gifts that God has placed in them and recognizing that; that their gift was not only for them, that the gift was giving to them for them to free someone else and through their prayers, teachings, fasting, and counseling they have blessed not just one, but a congregation. This is not to worship them, but we all need to know that we are appreciated as a person for the feeling of accomplishment, and why not make them be let known. Please do not stop the walk of faith, because acknowledgment is what keeps some of us going. An emotional reward is not so bad every once in a while we all need something to continue in the work that we do; even pastors are human and believe it or not they need to be told more than us the more they preach and pray the more the devil attacks. They need the strengthening; as well as, lifted in the spirit, because the devil attacks them most.

<u>Heart-To-Heart</u>

I haven't known you long, but I feel like it's been forever your like the Father I had never.

Words can't express the appreciation I have for you, to preach and pray for our souls the way you do.

To Listen to your calling that you will fulfill that makes you a great leader to yield your will.

Some knows not what it means what love your heart holds inside, but Bishop Willie Lamb the Sims family appreciate you. I encourage you, cause for me that's what you do.

WE LOVE YOU

If You Hadn't Reached Me first speaks of being lost in sin; even in that sin; they weren't being passed around like a prostitute. In the eyes of others this young lady was promiscuous and abused herself along the way with partners she choose to lay with. When she identified what state she was in she got out; not wanting to live that way anymore. This young lady started to cut her blessings and faced what she had coming her way. She knew what waited for her; when she was ready to live right. Old habits are embedded they are hard to break. She put her priorities in order; wanting the gifts of heaven and turning away from sin and seeking first the kingdom of heaven and all it's righteousness so that her land could be healed. Nothing was offered better to her than the Father, The son, and The Holyghost.

If You Hadn't Reached Me First!

Where would I be if you hadn't reached me first,
Alone and in someone's hands who would have hurt me,
Mistreated, used, and abused me.

See yes! All of that did happen to me, but I got out before it
could even began to get major and those were some of the wrong
choices that I made.

We get to choose life or death according to the Holy Bible,
only I chose death, but without an appointment, life was sitting;
on the back row.

I could have been in someone's harlot home as the bible says
giving my pearls to pigs, for something real cheap anything other
than the lord, no matter what it maybe even a million dollars is even
cheap when it comes to your body. Your just fragmenting your soul
go for the expensive stuff like the Holyghost, eternal life, salvation,
redemption and all that comes with giving yourself to him.

Be sold out to Jesus there's nothing more expensive than he nor,
what he has, because when you think about it the millions come with
him. He's the one who has it and holds all things and power in his
hands.

May I Lay At Your Feet?

*Lord May I lay at your feet and just worship you not
to ask and beg you for anything, but to give you reverence.*
*Tell you that I'd love to learn your ways, so you may search my
heart, make me pure. Clean my spirit as I lay in your presence and
feel your anointing, one on one, feel you through my soul.*
*Just for a washing of your Holyspirit to be made whole. To wake,
and see you early in the morning, and wash your feet with my tears;
Just surrendering to you and whatever you want for me to do.
'When I lay at your feet. I'll know just what to do, because I will hear
with a spiritual ear. What the Holyspirit has to say and let it lead,
and guide the way. May I tell you that I love you, I don't ever want
to leave you. I hurt sometimes and get side tracked, and go the
opposite way, but I always keep you in mind and in heart, and not
ever forgetting who you are or what you have done and never, never
forgetting to tell the people of your goodness.*
*So even when I am away I still keep you in mind and want to lay at
your feet. I hold grudges and I know that is where, I'll get my
deliverance when I lay at your feet. Weeping may endure for a
night, but joy comes in the morning, you never fail to show it and
grateful, am that it's all taken care of at your feet. Time that is not
one minute wasted, it's all quality time with you and it's worth time
with you and it's worth spending.*

Intimate Struggle's expressed the missions that had to take place in order to pull things back together. This poem tells a tale on behalf of a young lady feeling her way through the dark, and making it the best way she can as a single mother and having five children in foster care and one still in her care that never separated from her; went to work with her, the young ladies second hustle was to do braids on the side, so when she'd come home she would get that child prepared for bed and work the night doing hair sometimes the money fitted the bill for her transportation to and from work. Some hustles spoke of what other young ladies had to do, but we all realize at some point God is the one that judges us, because in any situation they were being judged; by on lookers (neighbors and always the bloodline). Knowing your down fall is best, because knowing is half the battle; that was the best piece of advice I'd ever gotten. This particular piece exercises the devil seeing who this person was and sent temptation, because he knows your weaknesses. What will get your goat; so he sends your temptation for your down fall, but God in all knows us as well better than the father of lies. As a people we think with carnal minds that there is a war going on between God and the devil, "but God" is in total control. Even in the fight of struggling with that are not your choice of sin, but the choice is yours God gives you the strength to fight and he always gives us a way of escape it's up to us to see the way of turning away. (it's our decision)

Intimate Struggles

For my maturity for understanding only I know what
they have purpose for at the end get understanding.
Only I feel my pain, cold nights on my mission
from work carrying my precious load of a baby, this was on
a daily basis never no maybe.Wondering where was my sperm
donor? Somewhere in the process of making another baby claiming
neither knowing he's the owner. Going home checking the calendar
for my second hustle, Stopping the third one, because in God's eyes
I'll be the personWho won, besides doing that I felt I was in a bind.
Dealing with the spirit of fear wasn't a good thing when God
Said he didn't give me the spirit of fear, but of power, Love, and of a
sound mind. No one said it was easy, but when you go from nothing
to something it's easier to appreciate desperate for money the devil
saw me and sent evil fishermen,Who used bait. Money not worth it,
but they had up front rate. Couldn't do it Right away so we set a
date. Dealing with soon to come emotions, fear, Anxiety, and others
to put in this category of variety. I do my best to talk to God and get
my emotions back to where they should be. Seeing everything I need
to do when putting it in perspective it's a wonder If I'll make it
through, but lord I know we will cause it's just us, me and you No.1
in this plan and my struggles have, yet to begin, still, Please! don't
let me pick up on drugs or gin and I can probably Look and see in
my years of aging around the bend. On my way I know your love
you'll send. Not like evil that ones from majority of these men
(women) Looking for a piece of my body for me to lend, I will or I
won't it's up to me, whatever my answer is, just what it will be

Does This Mean illustrates of asking god exactly what does this mean, because I don't understand why? I'm going through . I've heard people say don't question God, because your not suppose, to question him, but in his word it clearly states you have not, because you ask not and that is what his word says. I personally feel that if we are going through trials and tribulation who else do we ask another human being; who has no clue in what's going on in their life, so we spend aimless time wondering what's going on and never finding an answer, because people say don't question God which contradicts his word, because in another part of the bible it says in all of your getting get understanding. I believe that these are the things that keep us blind and bound up. When we backslide knowingly we back away from the table that he has prepared for us and our convictions eat away at our conscience along with the persecutions of people that are watching us and waiting for us to fall, but he gives us a way back to repentance and to move on. He says also in his word that when you fall into divers temptation to count it all joy. My personal opinion is, because you learn from your mistakes. We have so many questions but old tells advises us not to question God, but when asked why they say I don't; I was just told not to question him. Well I give you this example when you are going through somewhere and you need to find the way; before Gps we stopped in the gas station or store and asked how to get there (we asked for direction). Now that we have gps we pull it up on our navigator and gps gives the address and it leads us right to the place. Once again when we pray and ask questions we are asking for direction on how to get there from where we are now and so we charge the angels of God to give him our prayers and we get answers an results, by asking questions like Lord Does This Mean?

Does This Mean

Dear Lord,

I know I've done wrong and I still have not lived to your total and complete standards according to your word; so Does This Mean you don't have anything to do with me? I know I haven't kept my promises to go to the places that I said I would go and minister to the people that you would allow me to. Lord does this mean that the opportunity has passed and you've found another, to do it and my job no longer stands. What I really want to ask you is since you have given the children back to me and a home to go with it, speaking that I was about to be evicted and you put me in a house so Does This Mean; that you forgive me? And I will have a second chance out of the plenty chances that I have already had and been forgiven for, even though man hasn't forgiven me does this mean that you have? Does this mean that what I use to take for granted that just won't do it anymore and I'll cherish your every word. What this means is I need to hear from you Lord and since I direct the children's choir and you are my help does this mean? I am accepted back into the Kingdom. Dear Lord if you can hear me can you please tell me is this what this means. Does Tlhis mean? Every gift that you have placed in me will be used regardless of how many times I have walked away Lord can you Please! tell me

Just keep me going illustrates an out pouring to God, asking him to use me keep me and anoint me for his use and never let me go unto the things that keeps me bound. Asking for his power to abide in me, as long as I abide in him, asking that the spirit of fear not to be within me as his holyspirit, gives me boldness, Asking him for his power, love and a soundmind. This is the illustration of the lord being the king he is and showing me through the years. One thing I noticed about when you come in contact with the Holyghost is that even in your backsliding the spirit imprints on your soul and you are never the same even in your backsliding

Just Keep Me Going

Lord just keep me going in you and never without if there's one thing after another I don't have time to sit with idle things on my mind. Lord just keep me going in your ways and doing your work keep my feet moving in what you want me to do use me Lord and Lay your anointing on me so I'll slip no more keep me young and in good health keep me going in you let the strength grow greater with you and help me to endure. Let my vision become very much so clear let your power abide in me as I abide in you let not fear steer me, but the power of love, and a sound mind.
THANK YOU LORD FOR YOUR SPIRIT IT GUIDED ME RIGHT ON TIME.

My Vision And Me

I have a vision of living free soaring through the sky with clouds, So beautifully pictured blue. I would be as mellow pure as a dove. My wings gently spreaded flowing in the win, as I'm up held by my feathers no eagles to sweep; down and see me as prey. Above everything else looking at my life in my past along with my thoughts, my privacy, my dignity, my peace, also my conversation with God, not trying to hear everything he says only what I want to hear. As slowly I go for a landing. I come out of my vision reality starts to kick in. All over, I'm me once again dealing with my hard to kill emotion, and my bogged down thoughts thinking the worst of everything, but all and all the ball is in my court and it's the way I handle it is what keeps me being me; No matter what way, I shoot it in the hoop, only I can make a decision of whom I am. Because I'm still me and that's the deal on how it will be.

This is the day speaks of hardships; and yet saying thank you lord. Looking to you what may appear to the natural eye to be suffering as if you will always be thanking God for your whoa it's me days. Although you know he's the same today, yesterday, and forever; he is not a switch a roo God; you can't put him in a box. A lot of our short coming comes from us and if we would only listen we would hear him saying come unto me, but it's hard to accept what we've done, because we look for God to fix what we've messed up so when thins happen it only leaves us to blame who is blameless. Just think who you take out your problems out on: the person closest to you. He takes our tears and bottle them up in a jar remembering what they are for we must count every down fall as a blessing in his word the King James version he tells us that when we fall into divers temptation to count it all joy, your every down fall will be your best design of your new makeover. this is the day speaks of seasons those are the seasons that come like; summer, spring, fall, and winter: the season we experience as a people are a season to cry, a season to laugh, etc. The moral of this is the day in all things give thanks even when it's all closing in on you and it seems like there is no way out. That if you just hold on wait on God be obedient all that you lack will be brought to you and he when you say this is the day it will be your day.

This Is The Day

No matter what or how you think it went; This Is The Day, that the Lord has made and how may have to walk around with no money in your pocket and no food to ear and watched everybody else eat, do fun thing, ride around in their fancy cars, and pass you by; I know that is one hard thing to do, but this is the day that the lord has made. We will rejoice and be glad in it for we know weeping may endure for a night, but joy comes in the morning and we must not forget that and hold on to what the bible tells us, because it's true and unfailing, I know I have tried god in some ways and he is unchanging. You may have listened to the lord tell people a prophecy and they babble on about what God has done for them and tell you all his wonders and you can't think back to when the last time he did something for you and still you've sent your night or, maybe even your day crying all alone

And no one understands, but talking to the love of your life even then could not understand wasn't in them to comprehend what was even being said and the spirit wasn't in them to even discern what the spirit would have for you to hear. It just seems like all hope was gone, but guess what this is the day the lord has made we will rejoice and be glad in it the cloths you wore and been wearing, because you didn't have the money to go to the thrift store, and purchase you a suit for church and the pair of jogging pants you've been wearing just isn't getting it anymore, you lost your job, the children have been wearing them shoes since sister so and so gave them to you last year, you can't pay the rent, at food banks looking for your next meal, this is the day that the lord has made we will rejoice and be glad in it.

There is a due season you walk in the church and a member tell you they are hiring at her job for a supervisor position and you tell her that you don't have the skills for the job and the lord tells you to go and you question is this really the lord, but following the Holyghost you walk into that office with confidence stands up in your soul, answer the questions asked of you to the best of your ability, and continue to stand on faith; with God's angels fighting for you and your position, it comes down to the application and they still hire you with no experience and you know; this is the day that the lord has made. The job begins and you maintain your position, here comes the new house that you have wanted, being able to provide and not having to wait on sister so and so to give you things, and now you help those that are going through a season and need help alone the way; So truly you know, this is the day that the lord has made. Your husband has watched life grow around him and now knows this is the day that the lord has made.

I don't receive it speaks of negative spirits, actions, and people that are used by old(familiar) spirits you use to have trying to get back in. Rebuking the devil pushing him and his imps out my way whenever, you fight the devil, you must fight him with prayer, scripture and the confessions from our lips of our faith. We do not need much to please! Him(God) A grain of a mustard seed is all we need, but our actions dictate our belief "actions speaks more volume than words" refusing to believe the report of the enemy and taking your innerman spirit and battling down what is going on around you speaking to that demon calling it by name and letting that demon know it has no power over you, that you are a child of God. Speak those things that are not as though they were and this illustrates I don't receive it.

I Don't Receive It

I've been here before and I'm not walking through that door. I don't believe in it and I don't receive it I say no to Anxiety (panic attacks). No fear for me; God has not given me a spirit of fear, but of power, love, and of a sound mind. I refuse to accept the fear of dying, though I walk through the valley of the shadow of death. I will fear no evil for though art with me.

I press pass your assumptions devil telling me that my peace is gone, get behind me satan for the Lord keeps me in perfect peace. I won't listen to you tell me that my prayers won't be heard, because the lord told me in his word Matthew Ch.7 V.7&8 ask and it will be given to you , seek and you will find, knock and the door will be opened.

I give up on doubt you said if I had the faith of a mustard seed that I could move mountains. Negative speaking is not part of my vocabulary, in your word tells me my words are life and death. I'll say no thanks to fornication I have better things to do than to get ungodly soul ties.

What's Change speaks of the metamorphosis of life: learning to go through finding the better of you. Explaining the meaning of change, because everyone does not know exactly what it means to change, they know that something about themselves is different. The actual and foresure meaning of change- is the cause to become different to alter, transform, convert, leaving old things behind and all things becoming new. This illustration is a product of repentance and not giving up on what you believe God and your heart has given the version for you. Turning a negative to a positive following of the teachings of your hearts, desire; finding happiness and letting go of depression through your actions, uplifting your personal being for pride, but for you not to walk in God and making you whole; meaning the transformation has taken place, not still in conversion, but mission is well accomplished. What's change is a makeover of yourself for a better you.

What's Change

Change is a difference in a thing. To switch from one way to another, Never turning back, to that thing or old way. The actual and for sure meaning of change is to cause, to become different, to alter, transform, convert, leaving old things behind and all things becoming new. Changing is a process of the motion, but change is from something bad to good or vice versa choose ye life or death.

Saying you have a choice to choose. To be changed is never turning back from whoredome; to virtuous woman, or evil to good, ignorance to wisdom, from slow to advanced, from filthy to cleansed, from unfaithful to faithful, from gossiper to blesser, from dessert to green pastures, from wrath to mercy, from death to life, from sinner to saved children of God, hearts from hate to love, from greed to satisfaction, from narrow minded to the mind of Christ, from weakness to strength, from poverty to riches; King James says in Proverbs 23: 4 labor not to be rich, cease from thine own wisdom. From depression to freedom, from fear to faith, Isaiah 41:10 fear thou not for I am with thee: be not dismayed; for I am thy God; I will strengthen thee; yea I will uphold thee with the right hand of my righteousness. We shall not all sleep, but we shall all be changed, meaning the transformation has taken place, not still in conversion, but mission is well accomplished.

Not in my own strength, but yours calls upon God and his Holyghost for strength, because no strength came from within me looking for love, and money making all else not so important, because survival was more important one more time; putting God on the back burner. time away from God has me picking up bad habits, that I was delivered from and picking up new bad habits: in the backslide I picked up worrying, but on a deeper level of anxiety had me feeling like I wanted to hurt myself. In Matthew ch:7 V6 give not that which is holy unto dogs. Neither cast ye your pearls before swine, lest they trample them under their feet, and turn again and rend you realizing that distance between God and myself has me wanting to know him once again looking to be picked up dusted off and cleaned up. I knew I needed God he has always accepted me back and loved me and I've often heard God has to draw you well. I feel the pull at my heart all the time; as if he's always calling me to him even in my wrong doing he called his periodical daughter. I only made my way back to him, because Lord I believe I can accomplish anything only not in my own strength, but yours is all I need to help me fight off weakness indeed.

Not In My Own Strength, But Yours

Lord, father in the name of Jesus help, because I can't do it all in my own strength Yes! I'm ready to say good-bye, to all those things I told you about, but not in my own strength the men I cheat with on a weekly basis I can't say no not in, my own strength.

To not worry is an, amazement in my own strength, but not in yours. Lord, in Matthew ch.7-v.6 give not that which is holy unto the dogs neither cast ye your pearls before swine, lest they trample them under their feet, and turn again and rend you. Rend means to tear, pull apart, rip up, or split with violence often use figuratively. Lord, I heard often that I would need, well if so please! Be my strength.

I want to work my way back to you. My strength is drained and gone it's separate ways so I can't in my own strength, but yours, besides you said you were my refuge, a safety net for your children.

Lord, I believe I can accomplish anything only not in my strength, but yours is all I need to help me fight off my weakness
INDEED.

Ready to Say goodbye is an expression of leaving all the worldly things behind that had introduced theirselves to me and with my acceptance, attached to me for a day to day practice of those very things that I knew my father did not want for me to have played out. The key to being saved is that you are not saved for yourself you are saved for the safety of other individuals and to bring souls into his kingdom for him, and instead of bringing them in they were being maintained in a dry place of sin and hindered for the sake of the enemies purpose.

<u>*Ready To Say Good Bye!*</u>

Ready to say good-bye to the night clubs of
Seduction, the gyrating of my hips,
the endless licking of my lips selling my dope,
I just told the children in that there
was no hope. To the diaherra of fornication, I don' want
to end up in hell plus to say I had no heavy sedation
too-da-lou, foul speaking. In the name of Jesus,
I curse every word against those I spoke upon them you won't do
any creeping. Good-bye to my deceitful planning and my wicked
Ways, saying after while to all those evil days.
Although, the devil will still chase and send out his
Imps. I refuse for my body and soul for you to be my pimp
See you later to all those old friends with familiar spirits
This is where the boat stops I'm letting you off my
Dearest. I picked you up and now I'm letting you Go
Wait just a minute don't step to quick, here's your luggage, I'm done
with it. I know you think I'm being cruel, but I want what God
Has for me and this is one of his rules. I'm ready to say good-bye I
must say it's a pull, but I want to walk away and see the
devil drool. He slobbed all over me with his mischief
Now he'll choke on his evil for my firm belief.
Saying good-bye is not an easy thing for the old ways,
Come out of habit. Farewell to impatience and poor endurance
peace to the devil and his entanglements. I looked
In the green pastures and I didn't see you there.
I'm ready to say Good-bye and I'll drop you right
Here!!!

Women don't settle for less gives the illustration of what women go through on a life time basis dealing with men, other women, climbing a ladder of success is not an easy one to climb with dreams and ambitions; with obstacles by your own doing and then the other half is like crabs in a pot; if I can't achieve neither can you and even if I don't want to achieve I surely don't want you to so take these bricks of distractions start to fly, but ultimately your success is on you. We must know when the enemy is at work; identify him and knock him down with the biggest blow that our God given talent will bring up and out women and men for that matter Don't settle for less.

<u>Women Don't Settle For Less</u>

We've had our hardships of this man and that man,
But because of our wrong doing, we must suffer even
greater prices, plus the hurt of what we've encountered
and the endurance of what others have to say even after
then! We're not valued or valuable in many ways to men thought
less of, because we deal with or maybe even the company
we keep, the way were dressed if a lot of sexual advances come
your way check you out first; and see just what is drawing them
we were not chosen to be played with and have a sign that says
tampered and thrown to the side.
God has plans for us and we have a destination. God knew us before
the foundations of the world. Women lying with other women; it's
an abomination to God. Degrading ourselves with
the same gender, children being confused and really not knowing
the difference, at a later age.
We're held accountable for our sins, that will be passed down
From generation to generation, because of what we want and not
thinking about God or our children. We have it hard enough as
women than to settle for more self-inflicting heart ache use one
another get all out your hook up, because someone else is sleeping
with that man or woman that told you they were all yours and did
what they wanted to do; it isn't yours never was and never will be,
unless it was ordered by the Lord.

Lord I'm Almost

Almost giving up, almost giving in at the
end of my rope where I choose to hang in.
Almost there, but I feel like turning around.
I can almost see you although, I feel your presence
a bit you're here and that's what counts,
Still telling me not to quit.
A winner never quits and a quitter never wins.
Almost doesn't mean I'm throwing in the
towel, my definition is to the devil
completely I choose not to bow.
Almost is failure turned inside out,
But for you to let me give up that I surely doubt.
Almost at your feet, but yet so quick to sin
This one thing I appreciate is lord you don't bend.
So much to do, so little time to do it,
All the wrong things here I stand in dispose
All the while from your windows and doors
my blessing still flows.
It's been a journey, but still there not closed.
I almost lost sight in your spiritual light,
even in the day it seemed like night.
I almost couldn't see you, but you saw me,
And I know that's what got me through.
I almost accepted everything the devil had for me,
But your eyes ran to and fro in the earth
And you said not my child that just couldn't be.
The devil almost had me: I could have been lost in his
Bout.
But you tapped me on the shoulder and said Bessie
ALMOST DOESN'T COUNT.

Am I Speaking From My Heart?

To tell you how I feel in anger or express myself
In hateful words, to say I want revenge,
To see another hurt in pain and
agony right before, my eyes, God Please tell me
am I speaking from my heart? Because that's just a start.
I'm suppose to want to bless and not deal with the silly mess, but
call on your name when I start feeling to offend someone, to
want to hurt them to no end, when I need to let go of lost of words,
but can't explain the anger I
have when the pain I feel seems as an open wound that has been
picked at and knows no way or even the action to take of
healing the open sore.
Tell me where do I start or are to you my words a bore.
I don't believe they are, because you know more than I ever
Could and your mercy and grace you show, I speak those things
from within, because I must put the devil on front for him thinking
he can get by and send me constantly through and emotional stunt.
So I push and I'll force him to give me the victory as I pray in
Secret and give God praise then he will reward me openly
Not stopping at my distractions is won and come on with life
with everything in my heart. I won't give up and I will not give
In, even when I've fallen pray and ask you to help and ask your
spirit to push me from within.

Draw Me Again I Pray

I have heard through the years, you can't cone to the lord,
unless you be drawn and Lord your word tells me that any-
thing; that I ask the Father In Jesus Name that you will do it.
I believe what you have said to me from your word, so draw me
Lord. One more time pull your will from the depths of my soul
and let your spirit rain in this vessel. Let the bells of peace ring
in my inner man, let joy be my strength and let that be my gas and
refill me when needed, every time I give it out please! put more back
in. Let me hear you call my name in the middle of the night to say a
prayer, draw nigh to my heart and let your spirit rain, fluently
throughout my soul through your Holy Spirit.
Let your word bring me to the newness of you; it tells me in the King
James version of your word is like a lamp unto my feet and a light
unto my path! Let me be spiritually fed with the word. While your
eyes go to and fro in the earth I hope and pray that they are looking
for me being drawn and succeeding in what you have left for me to
do. Help me Lord to walk in the
right steps ordered by the Lord. Let the noise of Angels surround me
saying hallelujah giving the highest praise, usher my thoughts back
to you on the way to recovery and redemption, resurrect my soul
bless me in every way for a spiritual renewal.
Draw me to do a 360 degree turn toward you and full force in your
ministry push my back against the wall and cup my heart with your
spirit let my cry say every bit of I want you and you only draw me
to thirst for you as a woman thirst for her husband or a plant thirst
for water, draw me never to be satisfied with being in a comfort a
zone. Draw me to the realness of God the father, the son, and the
Holy Ghost! Draw me Lord Draw me at any cause so that you'll say
well done! So Father I don't just ask, but I plead and beg Draw me
Again I pray.

Sometimes I Need You More

*When I wake up and my feet hit the floor my life is everything,
but a bore, my mind is racing and so is my heart beating just
as fast as it must, but I know that in you I shall put my trust.
Clenching on to you and your unchanging hand, as my soul plays
a joyful noise as if it were a Christian band some days are so dark
my nights even darker. I see you in the shadows, you come down in
the valley and visit me and visit me and I look to you and say Lord
God lee. How much can I take how much more can I stand. More
and more I guess I'll say, even when stress and depression, come my
way on my feet I will land. Sometimes I need you more. Especially,
when I am weak. When my walk on this straight and narrow
is so bleak. How much further do I have to go only time will tell and
only you know. Where I'll end up and what all will flow through this
vessel I know I'm something else, but I know I'm no hand full.
Sometimes I need you more just to slow me down, not only to get a
reward to wear a goldencrown. I refuse to except that my faith is
gone, because I asked the lord to let me walk to him and hear him
say well done. Help Me! To get rid of this doubt, Sometimes I need
you more just to give a holy shout. So I send this prayer and hope
you'll keep it in store and hope that you'll be there sometimes when I
need you more.*

Keep On Keepin On

*Here they come, here they are knock, knock, knocking at my door
No matter how many times he tries, coming with the same thing just
in a different way he never gets bored. Going to and fro in the earth
roaring like a lion seeking whom he may devour. When the bills are
due, disconnection notices come forth, just before they can cut them
off God shows up in that hour. When my flesh is weak and my soul
struggles within I cry to my father and tell him what's my bother he
gives me another dose of his spirit and fills me with his powers, as he
reigns his anointing over my head and washes me with a cleansing
shower. He tells me to keep on keepin on my spirit is within you it's
not gone. When the man that you Love is not walking the same walk
as you and you must go the opposite way your soul hurts along with
your heart. You need a broken and a contrite spirit here I am so
Lord do your part. When friends have forsaken you, because of a
misunderstanding and really, because the devil has got in the mix,
seem like he's won the battle so it seems like he's got his fix, but no,
no you keep on keepin on praying for the others for unity as one
accord for your sisters and brothers working out your own
salvation with fear and trembling, but you stand still and see the
salvation of the Lord watch him bring things together on one accord.
I'll ask the Lord to give me strength to stand in the gap. While your
brothers and sisters have gone astray leave them alone they'll
be back if it's only so that they can have rest for a peaceful nap.
Some feel as though we have to take what life has dished out, but
push past it and keep going no matter what we have to deal with we
must keep on keepin on!*

Just Invision!

Meeting at the church house after praising God high in the Holyghost my brother in Christ asks me would I like to go to a revival with him our relationship with Christ gets build up and our love grows for one another in him we're strengthened in his word and prayers are better heard when we kneel to pray together. Living happily ever after with someone you love and loves you back the same hoping the best for each, others well-being . Living in a house with a Pickett fence on a hill with green grass, white Persian cat, and the cocker spaniel' puppy; to chase the cat through the big front yard. The children chasing behind them me sitting and admiring my husband working in the yard and the children chasing the puppies and cats. The brief enjoyment of the envision makes me feel as if I'm there.

If I Let Go Now

If I let go I'll be turning my back on you Lord help me to hold on to all that you have for me to see your promises that were destined for my eyes only. How will I look my children in the face as they cross over to heavens doors, the love that Emmanuel has for me is so real and it could never run as deep as the Lords is for me ot saying he doesn't love me deep, but it could never go as deep as the Lord and Savior Jesus Christ we take it so lightly that he stretched out his arms wide and shed his blood on cavalry, but Lord people say it now, because it sounds right, but I pray this day as those words roll out of the mouth of those who speak it let them feel those words in their heats in the name of Jesus. So much I want to see and say to the world what the Lord has put in me I won't get to see that if I let go Now! I want to shout all over the church and tell of his goodness, grace and his mercy travel the world and tell about the love that he has for us. Watch the children that he has placed in my life grow, become something in you and make families together speak to my grandchildren and tell them about my God who delivers, saves, and sets free. Pray for them on their good days and bad ones too, how could I see this if I Let Go Now!

Leave Her Alone She's My Child!

Now that your back with me I can give you everything you desire in your heart; you said you wanted, according to my word; you said you wanted nothing without me. I understand you and because
I'm God doesn't mean I did not respect, your prayer and hopes when you left me; since it is not of me to be a respecter of persons, the door of blessings never closed. With a fresh start I will give to you the Holyghost; for wisdom and understanding then I'll provide you with the information that you turned away, so I'm opening the door to understanding and opportunity awaits you, it's your decision to walk through. I'll give you vision to victory, hope to dream, prayer and prayer language to fight. Ministering angles in the middle of the night to minister to you before you can lose sight.
I've got hold of and want you to know you'll be alright.

<u>Praise Me The Lord Your God!</u>

Praise Me! If you want to move me, then praise me.
Praise Moves mountains and confuses the devils mind
Praise Me!
Praise Me! The Lord Your God for you I went to the cross
shed my blood and my father gave you his best.
Praise me until you hear the heavens clap.
Praise me in the earth so that I may hear it from the heavens you
Were made for my purpose and you've been chosen so with all
your mind, body, soul, and might in your body that I breathed the
breath of life into praise me praise me praise me praise me with the
breath that I have given you.
Don't let rocks cry out in your place Praise Me!

Are The Rocks Crying Out?

Don't let no rock cry out in your place fill your space,
when you're the one who has a meeting with him
early in the morning face-to-face.

Don't let no rock cry out in your place, besides he said
Praise him in any case praise him when your up, praise
him when your down, praise your way out the storm,
praise him so your soul won't be torn.

Don't let no rock cry out in your place. Praise him with
your limbs, praise him in hymns, praise him even though
it's fact you don't have on the best of cloths, your toes hanging
over your timbo's, you can sit there I suppose, but one thing
is for sho aint no rock cryin out in my place. I'z gone praise
him like I'z crazy lost my mind and when I'z finish you'ze
gone think I'z drunk. I'z gone stager my way to heaven drunken
in the spirit. This here something I'z want the whole world to
hear it.

<u>Many Let Go's</u>

Let go and let God, you hear it all the time; well either
You let go or give up God.
Let go of that thing that keeps you bound.
Let go of that job.
Let Go of those cloths, means you no good.
Let go of the that jewelry that you did God knows what; to get.
Yes many let go's mean let go to that which your flesh loves.
Your spirit continues to tell you Let Go and let God.
Let go of that friend that keeps you gossiping on that phone.
Get you a godly one and leave that one alone.
For this is only some of the many let go's.

I'll Wait For My Mate

This May just be a fantasy,
but somewhere within me lies
hope for me and you
destined to be with one another, I
believe fait to bring it true.
See some people say that I've probably
Missed all my opportunities, but
God's just taking this time,
To bring through me loves sureties.
That I will be patient in who you are
and the laws you lay down and thus
far.
In our ways of talking it's blowing of the
Flowers I like the way and fashion of our
Communication, sometimes we speak with
Our minds, our love, respect, and honesty
Stands like twin towers.
Every time you enter my presence I get chills
As if I've taken a shower.
Baby Love me as Christ Loves the church
Hour up on the hour.
Make my mind stand pleasured in everything
that you do. I'll be so glad when I reach this point,
because so many people said that it can't come
true.
  The nights I lay in my bed and wonder who you were
I'd grab my teddy bear and slowly run my fingers
through the fur. My mind sends me through the scenes
of you loving me and me loving you this time
I know that I will be true.
I've had test to prove me of what I am saying to you
So there I will be served on a golden platter of preparation.

I will be so glad to see so
I can be free of loves starvation.
I won't get into what we'll do in the bedroom,
Because it could cause me to fall into
Fornication.
So I'll sit here knowing that this will come
true waiting with patients.

How Much More Lord

I'm speaking to you Lord out of what spirit or even in my flesh I don't know, but I have to get this out I have to speak to you about this ache, aggravation, and these things that dwell. I'm fed up and I want to deal, but I don't know how. I'm tired of being alone and dealing with these kids, I didn't make them alone. I need a real man in my life one with a back bone not laying up on me while I take care of him and the kids, One that's going to be right and bare the cross like Jesus did, it hurts me so much just looking in the children's faces when I think about how they let their backs turn and they ask constantly my expression show much disgrace. I want to be held someone to fight this battle with me. Laying with this man and that and when it's done and all over with I cry cause I laid on my back. I still wrestle with some old things and only you know. I know I'll deal with this hurt, but let me win and grow. I want what's best for me and you say you do too. We'll god where's my husband please! bring him through. I feel like running away and putting my problems on delay dealing with this everyday has made me go astray. The mentality I had before the children came back home, it's walked down the street and around the corner it roamed all these men coming my way I'm only a piece of meat. I want somebody to love me, but when they respond to me and I want to walk away, but my emotions grab me and say you know you need it so please! don't push me. I'm hurting and I'm looking for you to fix the situation you said your my father. I need help and I've run out of patience. When I deal with the man old enough to be my grand father and give him all my love when I stop calling he doesn't even call to see what's the problem. I feel used and abused like life has nothing more for me lord give a scripture except for hard times and struggles I don't feel like I see the breaking of day. I feel like I'm a walking dead man my body just haven't decayed.

Just What Are you Trying To Say To Me

Lord here I am where it seems that this question comes to me. I've been here before and I made it through crying in the midnight hour I know you caught and held my tears. In your glass bottle all through my yrs. Of crying out to you oh yes! My god he's mine. He'll see me through and one's to occur I'll get to see the devil drull. Past things have to rule, but I snapp back, kick, punch and send the angels to attack with their swords dipped in blood tell me how you can fight back, because he slack on you and your crap. Okay lord now it's you that I need to hear from I figure I ask you why? Am I still lying mens tendencies pain heart throbbing felt from me this was my first woman hood tragedies. Noooo this world cannot change me God made me who he says I am, I will be, you cannot take it from me HaHa HeHe I've once laughed at you land made my mind up that my heart will be one with thee. He gave me promises and those promised I will see the same words he spoke to Noah, Isaac, and David he passed it for the, and I see them so vividly you can't tell me that I have not become or coming closet to that proverbs 31 virtuous woman victorious I will be and on my way I'll walk by in the suttliest of laugh hem! You mad and tell you that's just what he's trying to say to me.

Beginning With Me!

I need a change, tired of doing the same. Feeling lonely need a man, you got time form me only need you for a couple of hours or even minutes or so. I have a need and you must fulfill it. Stress to let go and plans to take it out on you and a couple mo. You got some friends don't be, jealous I'm the one lonely, sad and depressed I may love you, but for you to deal with me, you must be blessed. Sent from heaven above, to put these demons under arrest. Don't send your friend my way to give me a small test, because I'll give him some and our relationship will be done. What I need from you: Stick by me love me through my trials, and temptations, stand with me and let me see through you loves manifestation. Huh! You think that's something just be steal and see what God has in store, he'll show me how to love you, because my heart has the desire, he don't want me to be no whore. I just need you standing with me us against the demons and the angels fight for us these evil swarming legions. When we finish with this test we'll be qualified for the regions we've come this far why stop now might as well jump the broom leave satan wondering how did we make it this far we seen what he's doing to the rest of the world and set ourselves apart. A match made in heaven that's what the one's in the world call us, I bet if you stop being funny, catch a hold, you'll jump on that same bus. See most of us can't see outside our fleshly needs every time you want to do right the devil got another trick up his sleeve, and He'll always make a way of escape, so try him, trust him, and believe; try the spirit by the spirit what he sent us for our comforter. He'll make you beautiful and it's not about just getting your hair done full body make over. **Beginning With Me**